MARTINA NAVRATILOVA
TENNIS POWER

MARTINA NAVRATILOVA

TENNIS POWER

BY R. R. KNUDSON

Illustrated by George Angelini

PUFFIN BOOKS

Many thanks to George Vecsey,
whose MARTINA is far more than a best-seller.

PUFFIN BOOKS
Published by the Penguin Group
Viking Penguin Inc., 40 West 23rd Street, New York, New York 10010, U.S.A.
Penguin Books Ltd, 27 Wrights Lane, London W8 5TZ, England
Penguin Books Australia Ltd, Ringwood, Victoria, Australia
Penguin Books Canada Ltd, 2801 John Street, Markham, Ontario, Canada L3R 1B4
Penguin Books (N.Z.) Ltd, 182–190 Wairau Road, Auckland 10, New Zealand

Penguin Books Ltd, Registered Offices: Harmondsworth, Middlesex, England

First published by Viking Penguin Inc. 1986
Published in Puffin Books 1987
Reprinted 1988
Text copyright © R. R. Knudson, 1986
Illustrations copyright © George Angelini, 1986
All rights reserved

Printed in the United States of America by R. R. Donnelley & Sons Company, Harrisonburg, Virginia
Set in Garamond #3

"Women of Our Time" is a registered trademark of Viking Penguin Inc.

Library of Congress Cataloging in Publication Data
Knudson, R. Rozanne, 1932–   Martina Navratilova, tennis power.
(Women of our time)
Summary: A biography emphasizing the childhood and youth of the women's tennis champion who
defected from Czechoslovakia in 1975.
1. Navratilova, Martina, 1956–   —Juvenile literature.   2. Tennis players—United States—
Biography—Juvenile literature.   [1. Navratilova, Martina, 1956–   .   2. Tennis players]
I. Angelini, George, 1951–   ill.   II. Title.   III. Series: Women of our time (Puffin Books)
[GV994.N38   1987]   796.342′ 092′ 4   [B]   [92]   86-30377   ISBN 0-14-032218-3

Contents

1

Born to Play

On a winter afternoon in the mountains, a little girl named Martina Subertova was skiing beside her mother and father.

Martina didn't mind the frosty wind. She didn't mind the spills she took in the snow. She was fearless in her movements. She was tireless. She listened to her mother explain how to ride the skis, how to stop and stay upright. She held her father's hand as they walked back up the hill. They sang and laughed together. Martina had as much fun going uphill as she did gliding to the bottom.

The sky darkened above these mountains of Czechoslovakia (say "Check-o-slow-váw-kee-uh") but two-year-old Martina wanted to keep on skiing. She loved the feeling of balancing, poling, turning—the feeling of her body moving. She loved the freedom of being outdoors, where there was space to move in every direction.

And most of all, she loved learning from her mother and father.

She couldn't have asked for a better teacher than her mother, Jana Subertova. Jana was a versatile athlete: a gymnast, volleyball player, cross-country skier, and downhill ski racer. She worked as a professional athlete, giving ski lessons each winter.

Jana's own mother—Martina's grandmother—had been a tennis champion, ranking as high as #2 among Czech ("Check") women during her career as an amateur player. Jana had grown up on an estate with its own tennis court, and she might have become a champion. But she gave up tennis because her father pushed her too hard to improve. Their lessons often ended in tears. Jana had begun skiing to get away from such scenes.

Martina's father, Miroslav Subert, was also a professional skier, good enough to earn a living as a ski patrolman. He had met Jana on the ski slopes, and after they married they lived in a ski lodge named

Martinovka, or "Martin's Place." They named their daughter for this lodge when she was born on October 18, 1956.

A healthy, smiling daughter! A snug home and enjoyable jobs! Life for Jana and Miroslav seemed to be as smooth as the snow around them.

But not really. Jana grew unhappy with her husband because he was extremely moody. He swung from being high-spirited to being deeply sad, for no reason that Jana could understand. He would sometimes laugh or weep without control. These swings in mood made living with him difficult, so Jana moved back to live in her parents' house. Later she divorced Miroslav.

Jana took Martina, now three years old, to a home of only one room in the town of Revnice, Czechoslovakia.

Ah, but the room overlooked an old tennis court and an orchard, with fields and hills in the distance.

This grand estate had once belonged to Jana's mother, but not anymore because Czechoslovakia had become a communist country in 1948. The new Czech government had divided the rich people's property among *all* the people. Several families had moved into the estate's house, and the grounds around it were partly used for vegetable gardens and partly overgrown with weeds.

Martina used the bumpy tennis court for a soccer

field. She practiced kicking her soccer ball against a cement wall. She climbed trees in the old orchard and rode a tricycle near the house. She also swam in a nearby river, and when the river froze, she ice-skated there and played hockey. She played hopscotch at school, ran races against other students, and rode her bike on the streets of Revnice. Once in a while her father would come visiting and take her skiing.

Sports! Martina loved them all because of the movement and the challenge to get better. She dearly loved ice hockey—the "most exciting" sport, she called it.

Exciting or not, hockey disappeared along with the ice when spring came and snow turned to slush on the hills. No more skiing. (If Martina had grown up in a colder country, she might have become an Olympic skier.)

The spring sun also dried the clay tennis courts of Revnice for a season of play. Now, every afternoon, Jana went to the town's tennis club, up the hill from home. Martina walked along with her mother to the club's "baby-sitters"—all those tennis balls rolling off courts, balls for the energetic little girl to chase and throw back to players.

It wasn't long before Martina and Jana made friends with one of the club's best players, a pleasant man with as much energy as they had: Mirek Navratil.

Mirek played doubles, with Jana as his partner. He gave Martina rides in the wheelbarrow he used for hauling fresh clay to the courts. (Players there helped take care of the club.) Soon Mirek came to their room to eat dinner, to take them to pick berries and mushrooms in the hills, and eventually to stay as Martina's stepfather. She called him her "second father." She didn't much miss her first father, for Mirek Navratil was a generous, devoted, and good-natured companion.

Jana's new married name was Navratilova ("Nav-RAH-tee-low-VAH"). In Czechoslovakia, wives and daughters put "ova" after the family name.

The family lived in Jana's room and were comfortable and happy, even though life in communist Czechoslovakia was without many of the necessities that are taken for granted in other countries. For example, the family had no hot water from a tap. Water for baths had to be heated on a fire. They had no car. Jana took the train to a town nearby, where she worked as a secretary. Mirek rode his motorbike to his job in a factory office. There was little money left after salaries had been spent on the family's food and clothes.

But there was tennis and more tennis on days when the courts were dry.

While waiting for her parents at the club, Martina hit tennis balls against a wall. She used her grandmother's old wooden racket, and she hit left-handed from the very start. She was not quite five years old.

"I loved to volley off the wall," Martina has said about her first moves as a tennis player. To volley means to hit the ball before it bounces, and Martina could do it for hours.

Hours became months in the warm weather, then breaks for winter sports, then summer again. Martina hit alone until that great day when Mirek led the six-year-old child onto a court for a lesson from him.

"The moment I stepped onto that crunchy red clay, felt the grit under my sneakers, felt the joy of smacking a ball over the net, I knew I was in the right place."

Martina knew it, and Mirek did, too. He recognized Martina's natural talent and was impressed by her eagerness to learn, her willingness to follow directions, and her persistence in trying again each time she missed the ball. Mirek believed that winning tennis depended on winning ground strokes (any stroke used to hit the ball after it has bounced). He knew Martina would master her ground strokes only by taking hours of lessons.

Fine, he'd be willing to teach her. He liked tennis almost as much as she did! It would be fun to play with a daughter who would soon be able to give him a great game.

Across the net stood a skinny child, small for her age, but with wonderful athletic abilities. Martina was agile, well-coordinated, and strong, with quick reactions and explosive power. (Power is strength plus speed.) She had good hearing, which, when trained, would tell her the force and spin of the balls hit in her direction. She had unusually good vision for tracking the ball through space.

Now her watchful eyes were turned toward Mirek. He taught her to hit forehand. (For lefty Martina, this was the ground stroke used to hit balls on her left side.) He worked on her two-handed backhand. (For Martina, this meant hitting the ball with her left arm across her body.) He taught her to use her speed to move into position for these ground strokes.

Martina's wonderful speed, plus her natural temperament, plus her experience of volleying for years alone, caused conflict with Mirek. Right from her first lesson Martina wanted to rush the net to hit the ball before it bounced on her side.

But Mirek was a tennis conservative. He preferred a game of ground strokes.

Yes, but Martina didn't like to stand around the base line (back line) waiting for the bounce. That style of base-line play seemed unexciting. It didn't come naturally to her.

Maybe Martina was aggressive on court because she'd been a skier first, and skiing isn't a sport of waiting to move. A skier must aggressively attack the snow to get going. A skier must be willing to risk falling flat in order to move faster and better.

Early in life Martina had learned to attack and take

her chances in a sport, and now she did so in tennis.

At the tennis net there were many more chances to make sudden, dramatic hits than at the base line. But there were also more chances to make bad shots or to miss the ball completely—chances to fall flat.

So Martina's lessons were tugs-of-war between the conservative, ground-stroking Mirek and the "killer-shot" little girl. Martina would often fall flat, but Mirek avoided stormy scenes about her errors. He didn't want Martina to give up serious tennis, as Jana had given it up. And Martina herself was an intelligent student who, lesson by lesson, realized she needed good strokes on every inch of the court.

With some yells and some laughs, Martina compromised with Mirek in working toward their goals. Their lessons were mostly fun for both of them.

Mirek loved and admired his stepdaughter. He wanted a better future for her than his own life as a humdrum factory worker in a country where there were few chances to prosper and advance. Mirek also began to see himself covered with honor as the coach of a future star. He planted the idea of stardom in Martina's mind during lessons and gave her the distant goal of winning the world's most important tennis tournament.

Mirek hit balls to Martina, saying, "Make believe you're at Wimbledon."

2

Tennis Behind the Iron Curtain

Tennis in the suburb of Revnice was controlled by the weather. There were no indoor courts. After an autumn game Martina left her racket outdoors and didn't recover it until the spring thaw.

So much for tennis that year!

Tennis in the capital city of Prague was closely controlled by the government. The Czech Tennis Federation had chosen a former champion, George Parma, to coach at Prague's only public club with indoor courts. It was his job to discover and to teach players who could win tournaments all over the world, tournaments like Wimbledon. These winners would give the Czech government a good reputation in sports.

Martina came to George Parma for a tryout when she was still an undersized kid, nine years old. She had traveled to Prague by train with Mirek. He wanted her to have a chance to practice tennis year-round and to be coached by a pro. Wisely, Mirek had decided that some of Martina's skills now went beyond his.

"Don't worry, she's good," Mirek told George Parma just before the tryout. Mirek praised Martina to everyone who would listen.

His praise gave Martina self-confidence, which made her eager and loose on court. She slammed her trusty racket into some practice shots and then set to work running down the balls that George hit to her side of the net. He watched her scramble for fifteen minutes—twenty minutes—this tryout was longer than most! Scrawny kid or not, Martina had the right strokes. After thirty full minutes of hitting, George said, "I think I can do something with her."

This cool statement led into an important relationship in Martina's life: the ex-champ began coaching the next champ. Martina now rode the train to Prague once a week for her private lesson with George. Together they worked on changing her two-handed backhand to a one-handed backhand so she could reach balls farther away. George also taught Martina new shots. He taught her proper manners to use during tournaments. He suggested tactics for tournament matches. (A match is made up of sets of games. To win a match in women's tennis, a player must win two of three sets.)

George Parma stayed calm during lessons. He asked Martina to play the base line more, yet not to abandon her net game. He never screamed at her. And he never asked to be paid for teaching Martina.

"After a few lessons I would have walked through fire for this tall, handsome man," Martina has said, not cool like her coach. She was growing up to be emotional.

Opposites attract. Martina thought of Coach Parma as being "like a god." She thought of herself as a funny-looking kid, with huge feet and ears, with short hair and a skinny body that made her seem boyish. Not that she cared much. Her mind was usually on playing winning tennis. Winning made her feel "independent and self-confident," she says now.

Almost everything, including schoolwork, came second to tennis in Martina's life. She rarely studied, but still she managed to make excellent grades. She had one favorite class—not gym, but geography. In her gym class Martina was so far ahead of others, including the teachers, that she was bored. In geography she could sit back and dream about traveling to the places in her textbook: Australia, Japan, California, Miami Beach, the Empire State Building.

George Parma fueled her dreams with stories of his own tennis trips to faraway countries. Down deep inside, Martina began to feel that her sports ability would provide a way to see the world.

After a tennis lesson Martina would stay the night in Prague with her beloved grandmother Subertova. They'd eat supper and listen to music on the radio. They'd do crossword puzzles together. Martina would practice her school German on her German-speaking grandmother. Then little "Martinaka" would fall asleep on the couch and dream about the American movies she'd seen in Prague, the Westerns and musicals. She'd dream of meeting real cowboys and Indians, dancers and singers in America.

Such quiet times with her tenderhearted grandmother gave Martina a change of pace from the hurly-burly tennis world.

She'd already begun playing tournaments in distant Czech towns and cities. Her star was rising. Tennis officials had noticed her as a promising junior and welcomed her to their clubs. She rode to matches, perched behind Mirek on his motorbike, then rode right home again to work with him on her mistakes. Her mother had dinner waiting and didn't grumble about this way of life Martina was choosing over something more "normal." Jana willingly let Martina find her own role.

This close-knit family (it now included a baby girl named Jana) made sacrifices for Martina's tennis. For example, they saved money all winter for her travels and tennis rackets and tennis clothes and whatever Martina needed to become a winner in the summer.

Her family was Martina's team. Her first team.

A trip to West Germany proved the most exciting one during Martina's early years in competition. At age twelve she was the youngest player on the Czech team, yet she trounced the older West German players. She won medals and got her picture in the newspaper. With money Mirek gave her, Martina took home gifts of felt-tip pens, rarely seen in Czechoslovakia. She gave these to her sister and her school friends.

Martina's freedom to travel made her a celebrity at school. Such freedom was given to few Czechs. The western border of their country was lined with guard dogs and soldiers patrolling behind a high barbed-wire fence called the "iron curtain" because of its strength to keep people behind it.

No one left Czechoslovakia without government permission. Those who managed to sneak away were not permitted to come back.

Martina had been impressed by the freedom and

riches she had seen in West Germany. People there seemed to have plenty of money. They owned houses with running water. They owned cars. But even better, they could read, write, and say whatever they believed. They expected their government to help them live prosperous, free lives, and they criticized the government if it didn't help.

Czech citizens were afraid to grumble or to criticize their government. Their country was still filled with Russian soldiers left from 1968, when Russia had invaded. They'd come to "help" the Czech government put down "troublemakers." Martina well remembered the Russian invasion.

"A lot of us started tossing rocks and pebbles at the Russian tanks," she remembers about that day. Martina and her young friends reacted bravely but rashly. Czechoslovakia, a small country, didn't have a chance against huge Russia.

Not that Russia waged an all-out bloody war. The Russians moved in suddenly, swiftly, and without resistance.

In response to this invasion, 120,000 Czechs found their way out of Czechoslovakia. One of them was George Parma. So Martina lost her coach. Another who left was Martina's cousin Martin. He slipped across the border at a spot that wasn't guarded carefully. But other relatives of Martina's weren't tempted to leave.

They were cautious people who felt they'd be lost without their homeland and friends. They were content to "get along" where they were.

Martina's family was getting along better and better as Martina, once again coached by Mirek, rose in the tennis rankings. Her improving game earned her special favors. Her trips, and sometimes Mirek's, were being paid for by the Federation, which sent Martina to play in Poland, Bulgaria, Hungary, and East Germany. Martina's knowledge of the Russian language, acquired in school, helped her to notice the lack of freedom in those countries behind the iron curtain, where Russian was the second language.

Martina noticed, but she didn't protest about the restricted way of life. She didn't make waves. If she wanted to play at Wimbledon in England someday, she'd need help from the Czech government.

The Tennis Federation helped Martina join the Sparta Sports Club in Prague. At fifteen, she was now a member of the best tennis team in Czechoslovakia.

What a thrill to meet with this team every day! Martina spent mornings in high school, then rode the train to spend afternoons on the courts and in the clubhouse that became a second home to her. While waiting for court time, the teammates played chess and cards. They joked around, insulting each other as athletes do for fun. On court they took turns play-

ing each other, giving Martina a chance to hit against better players.

One of these was Renata Tomanova, two years older than Martina and a base-line player. Martina still played her serve-and-volley game. Her style was taking a long time to perfect, and Renata often put the ball past Martina at the net. But Martina continued to believe in her game. She looked ahead to a stronger, taller

17

body, to being able to slam the ball from her position in the forecourt. Then it would be harder for Martina's base-line opponents to return her hits.

At the Sparta Sports Club, Martina refined her doubles skill. A teammate, Jan Kodes, was at that time the best male player in Czechoslovakia. When paired with Martina in mixed doubles, he trusted her style of net play. He expected her to win her share of points and told her so.

"Jan Kodes treated me with respect when I was a little kid," Martina says of him. Such respect increased her belief in her serve-and-volley style.

Martina's singles game improved enough for her to win the Czech national championship in 1972.

Martina played at the nationals despite a bad cold. She just couldn't stay in bed. She made herself go out and hustle on court. She psyched herself up by thinking about the rewards of winning. Here was a chance to show the Federation that she was good enough to compete in international tennis. If she won, they'd let her play against the great women she'd been reading about in the tennis magazines her cousin Martin had been sending from his new home in Canada.

Billie Jean King. Margaret Court. Martina Navratilova wanted to play against them. She wanted to wear a beautiful tennis dress, the kind they wore in their photos in *World Tennis* magazine.

Meanwhile, in the Czech national finals, she won by beating Jan Kodes's sister.

Then Martina, sick with a bad cold, went home to Revnice for her mother's chicken soup.

3

Tennis Power

"She's only sixteen years old—she's from Czechoslovakia. . . ."

The tennis announcer's voice came over the loudspeaker, introducing a thin girl with hazel eyes, fine brown hair, and a wide smile. She waved in an energetic way to the crowd watching her take the court in Fort Lauderdale, Florida.

"Here's Martina Nav— Yes, it's Miss Nav-ra-til-ova. She's a new competitor on the circuit of the United States Lawn Tennis Association."

Martina was in America. And announcers had trouble pronouncing her name.

She'd been granted two months' vacation from high school. She'd been given her airplane tickets, a food allowance of eleven dollars per day, and a chaperone, Marie Neumannova, a fellow Czech player. The Czech Tennis Federation was depending on Martina to make a reputation for herself—and with no trouble at all, she did.

She earned honors with officials and players for playing fair and square, for being unwilling to score points on bad calls. If officials called a ball in (or out) of the court in her favor and she'd seen it otherwise, Martina cheerfully corrected them. She became popular with players also because of her wonderful language ability. This "foreigner," who already spoke three languages, now quickly picked up English.

American slang? No problem! Martina memorized the words to pop music she heard around the locker rooms and on the radio. She learned slang from TV programs she watched in hotels. She listened to fellow players talking at the clubhouses and learned from them. They helped her. Everyone was so friendly, Martina kept noticing.

Martina admired the American players' clothes. She liked their hairstyles. She loved riding in big American cars. She also appreciated the warm weather from Florida to Texas and back again. When she'd left home in Revnice, it had been icy winter.

Of all things American, Martina liked junk food

most. Or so it seemed on tour. She ate her first hamburger ever at a Fort Lauderdale tennis club. Then she ate another, another—and went on a "see-food" diet: she ate what she could see at Burger King, Wendy's, McDonald's, and other fast-food restaurants.

By the third week of the tour, she'd gained so much weight that a Russian player she'd known behind the iron curtain took one look at her and puffed out her cheeks without a word.

By the fourth week this "curvey" Martina (her own word) played a match against Chris Evert—their first meeting on a tennis court. Martina didn't think those extra pounds were the cause of her 7–6, 6–3 loss to Chris. Frankly, Martina rather liked her new curves.

By the last week on tour Martina was known as the "pancake champ."

"I cahn't beeleef I ate da whole t'ing," she said about an empty plate that had been stacked high. "I hof to borrow all new clothes. Even my feet get bigger."

In just eight weeks Martina gained twenty-five pounds. Her father didn't call her *Prut* ("stick") anymore when he met her plane at the Prague airport.

Her extra weight had been a handicap and would continue to be troublesome for years to come. Excess pounds use up energy to move around the court, energy that could better be used for long games, sets, and matches.

Yet just by playing aggressively until she tired, Martina won matches right from the beginning of her American tour. Tennis fans liked Martina's style: her powerful serves, her daring moves to the net. They liked to watch her chase down balls that most players wouldn't even try for. She could bash balls so hard she sometimes broke her racket. She didn't win tournaments in America, but her opponents began to take notice.

She showed them more—much more when she came to America again in 1974. This time she played as a professional on the Virginia Slims tour.

The cigarette company had organized eighteen tournaments for women, who would be trying to win a million dollars in Slims prize money. Martina and most other players weren't eager to advertise cigarettes by playing for Virginia Slims: players knew the harm of smoking. Yet they needed this chance to make a living from the game they loved.

Martina made a good living. She took home three thousand American dollars to the Czech Tennis Federation. That was prize money, and the Federation put it into their development program. There were other little girls coming along in Czech tennis: Hana Mandlikova, Helena Sukova. Martina's winnings helped support them.

Martina had saved most of her expense money by

eating free meals at the clubs where she played. Now, with that money left over from the pizza, Big Macs, and fried chicken she'd feasted on *between meals,* Martina bought her family a car—a Czech Skoda. What joy to be able to give them such an expensive gift! At last the family could travel together to see Martina play in Eastern Europe.

She used her time at home in Revnice to work on her backhand. She'd been losing points to players who knew how to take advantage of this weakness. Again Martina practiced by hitting to Mirek. With Jana's help, she dieted. She also did exercises to lose weight. When she returned to the American tour, she wanted to be slim and a winner, not just a candidate for Rookie of the Year, which *Tennis* magazine eventually named her, in 1974.

It was nice to be home, but Martina simply couldn't wait to fly back to America now that she'd found friends there. George Parma and his wife were living in New York. Other Czech citizens had been introducing themselves as Martina traveled from city to city. And her childhood tennis idols were nodding to her at matches, smiling, paying her small compliments. Who knows? Martina might even make friends with Billie Jean King.

Mirek and Jana were delighted with their daughter's success in America, but now they wanted her to stay home and finish high school. They thought ahead to the day when Martina wouldn't be winning prize money or even playing competitively. Then she'd need a high school diploma for a good job in Czechoslovakia.

Members of the Federation agreed that Martina should stay home. In their opinion she was getting "Americanized." Her slang, her new clothes, her friendships—these were all wrong. She should be spending her time with loyal Eastern Europeans instead of snubbing them. She must obey the Federation about coming home when they ordered her return.

Above all, Martina should remember that the Czech government—and the government alone—had the power to let her leave the country.

The Federation threatened. They had little "chats" with Martina and Mirek. But in the end Martina's tennis power got her out of the country in time to make the Slims tour and to play other tournaments in the winter and spring of 1975. The Federation gave in because it wanted the honor and money Martina's wins would bring them. American dollars were scarce behind the iron curtain. The Federation even consented to Martina's request, made through her new American business agent, to let her keep 80 percent of her prize money.

Martina won $200,000 playing tennis in 1975.

In tournaments she beat star after star. Virginia Wade. Evonne Goolagong. Margaret Court, whom she'd adored all during childhood. Martina made the singles finals of the Virginia Slims Championship, the French Open (open to professionals *and* amateur players), and the Italian Open. Martina even beat Chris Evert.

"That was the happiest day of my life," Martina said about her win.

A few weeks later she beat Chris again. They played so well, so fiercely every match they met—and still remained friendly—that they decided to be doubles

partners. Together they won four doubles championships in 1975, including the French Open.

All this glory—and still not enough for Martina to win every heart at home. Many Czech players and officials were jealous of her. They spread rumors that Martina would defect; she would leave her home country for good and ask for asylum (safety) in America if she ever had the chance to get out of Czechoslovakia again.

She was suddenly ordered to the Czech Sports Ministry and confronted with these rumors.

"I didn't want to defect, not totally. I just wanted to play tennis," Martina has explained about this time in her life. She denied the rumors. What else could she do with the officials menacing her with their power?

In fact, she had been thinking about staying in America. If she lived there, the Czech government could no longer tell her what to do. She believed their pressure made it hard for her to concentrate during matches. Her game would improve if she could only stop worrying about pleasing the Federation. Martina wanted to be the #1 player in the world, and for that she'd need her whole mind on her game.

On the other hand, if she defected, she would be separated from her family forever. Or so it seemed. She'd never be allowed to enter Czechoslovakia again, never see her childhood mountains, the old orchard around her Revnice home, her friends at the Sparta

Club. Her family might not be allowed to leave Czechoslovakia to visit her.

They, too, had considered defecting when they'd all been together in England, watching Martina play at Wimbledon in June 1975. But caution told them to go home. They felt they wouldn't be happy in America with Martina supporting them. Both Jana and Mirek were uncertain about jobs, friends, and positions in the American tennis world. They would miss their own power as minor tennis officials for the government.

What to do?

At the Sports Ministry Jan Kodes spoke convincingly about Martina's chance to win the U.S. Open in September 1975. Her win would be good for her country. With reluctance the Federation agreed and told Martina to come right back home after the U.S. Open.

"I had no idea when I'd get out again," Martina has said about their chilly tone. She packed her bag.

Her mother's good-bye was heartbreaking. She wouldn't let Martina tell her if she planned to defect. Jana wouldn't have been able to face the thought of never seeing Martina again.

Mirek was more practical. "If you're going to do it, stay there. Don't let us talk you into coming back," he told Martina for her own good.

Martina wasn't yet sure of her answer.

4

From #1 to #3

Martina became a public figure at the U.S. Open in September, 1975. No, not by winning. She lost to Chris Evert in the semifinals. But that night Martina asked the U.S. Immigration Service for asylum, and the next morning she found herself mobbed by TV crews.

Reporters pushed the eighteen-year-old Martina for a juicy story. They weren't satisfied with her answer— that she wanted freedom to play tennis when and where she pleased. They asked if she had an American boyfriend. If so, who? They asked about her politics. Would she remain a Communist? (No member of

Martina's family had ever belonged to the Communist party.)

And wasn't the Czech government embarrassed by Martina's defection? Would it seek revenge?

Martina began to wonder if the Czech secret police would try to kidnap her, stow her away on a jet, and sneak her back behind the iron curtain. Scary days were ahead. Martina moved from hideaway to hideaway with FBI agents guarding her. She played tennis while they watched from near the base line. The U.S. government was letting the world know that Martina's new freedom would be protected.

At a tournament in Denver, Colorado, the Czech coach, Vera Sukova, made one last effort to sweet-talk Martina into going home. Martina listened politely, shook hands, and said a firm no. She knew she'd end up in jail if she gave in.

"Navratilova prefers a fat bank account to a high school education," the Czech government declared in their newspaper. That was *their* end to her story.

The international tennis tour would be Martina's school from now on. Oh, maybe someday she'd finish her formal education. She admired the college tennis champions she played against during tournaments, and she sometimes hungered for their book learning. But there was so much else to be learned in her travels from the United States to Tokyo, Paris, Rome, London, Sydney (Australia), and back home to California. Martina scarcely had time to unpack and stay with the family of her business manager.

She was careful to choose airplanes that didn't cross Eastern Europe. If she'd been forced to land behind the iron curtain, she might have been taken into custody as a Czech citizen. It would be five years, according to U.S. law, before she could become an American citizen.

The life of a wandering pro suited independent, carefree Martina. Her real home became the tennis clubs, and her family the very women she competed with. Their locker room was their living room and dining room between games. They'd watch TV together. They'd try new hairstyles in the mirrors, try on each other's clothes and lipstick and perfume. They played Scrabble and backgammon. But mainly they gossiped endlessly about each other.

"Those huge muscles!" players whispered about Martina's strong arms. "Fat or not, she makes us look like we're in slow motion," they'd complain if they lost to her. Their gossip reached the newspapers.

"She's mopey. She's El Choko," Billie Jean King sometimes shouted about Martina. Billie Jean never whispered.

Martina was getting a reputation as a player who choked (panicked) when she muffed points. Lose a

few in a row—she'd blow a whole match because of her runaway emotions. She'd stand on court and weep about her mistakes. She'd yell "Stupid!" to herself between serves. Not in a playful tone of voice—the tone her heroine Billie Jean took when she scolded herself. Martina was being nasty to herself.

Off court, Martina's junk-food binges were puzzling to players. She'd eat whole quarts of ice cream in one sitting, then order a giant pizza delivered to the locker room—and "eat the whole thing." Most players were watching their weight. They found ways other than eating to comfort themselves after losing a match. They also watched their pocketbooks because they won less money on tour than Martina. Her shopping sprees were turning into locker-room legends.

She'd impulsively spend thousands of dollars on furs, dresses, sweaters, gold chains and watches, and on other beautiful things to wear. Then she'd wear only jeans and T-shirts. She also bought herself car after car, owning five of them at once. Her license plates said: "X-CZECH."

"The bouncing, happy Czech," sports articles still called her.

"Navrat the Brat," the players said, half in fun. They tried to tease Martina out of her sulks.

Billie Jean was usually the first to help Martina dry her tears. B.J. led the clubhouse "rat pack," playing her part as tennis guru to anyone who needed help. B.J. had done so much for women's tennis over the years. She'd been the only player who'd stood up and shouted for professional tournaments for women. She'd crusaded for cash prizes the size of those on the men's tour. All the players respected B.J., the "old" pro in her thirties and still playing, in spite of her sore knees. She organized her locker-room "Ladies" in rowdy tennis games late at night. They all wore outrageous costumes and took loony shots at the ball.

Martina clowned around with them. She liked being an entertainer. But next morning she might walk right past her friends without even looking at them. They called her "arrogant." They said her money had "gone to her head."

Years later, Martina explained her behavior by comparing her temperament to that of her first father, Miroslav, to his extreme moods. Like him, she wasn't able to control herself.

Chris Evert had other explanations: Martina's defection, the Russian invasion, Jana's divorce. "How many other teenagers have dealt with so much, so young?" Chris asked those who wanted her opinion of her moody doubles partner.

Their partnership helped Martina play some of her best tennis in 1976. That year she and Chris won the doubles championship at Wimbledon, making them the #1 women's doubles team in the world.

Becoming the #1 singles player proved to be much harder for Martina.

A complex system has been set up to decide #1 and to rank all other tournament players down to #300. This system depends on points earned. More points are earned by beating a high-ranking player than by beating a lower-ranking player. The more important tournaments award more points per game than do the smaller tournaments. In other words, games won at Wimbledon count for more than games won at a lesser tournament.

Wimbledon. "The Biggie"! Winning that English championship was always on Martina's ambitious mind when she should have been concentrating on the ball coming toward her in *every* game. She'd be hitting balls and dreaming about a future of wealth and fame. She'd be rushing the net and deciding which tennis dress to wear at Centre Court, Wimbledon Stadium. Martina knew that concentration was a tennis trait as important as her strokes. She knew better than to replay lost points over and over in her mind as she tossed up the ball to serve. But she'd go right ahead and replay her bad shots. She'd brood about bad calls from linesmen.

Let's face it: Martina needed help with her *mental* game. She needed the discipline and support—the coaching she'd had from her first family and later in the Sparta Club.

Martina turned to an older friend, Sandra Haynie. Sandra willingly gave up time in her own life as a golf pro to organize Martina's life. She helped Martina lose twenty pounds with diet and exercise. She taught the "pancake kid" to eat less junk food and more vegetables. Weighing less improved Martina's footwork. Being around such a calm homebody as Sandra caused Martina's game to settle down. She learned from Sandra how to concentrate on one point at a time.

Martina won six tournaments in 1977. "I got my confidence back," she told reporters. Her confidence carried over into 1978, to the finals at Wimbledon.

Throughout that entire two-week tournament Martina's mind was on the ball. Amazed reporters asked, "How do you keep your head together?"

"I stick it between the door and the frame in the locker room," Martina replied. Her wit helped her handle pressure.

After each win Martina phoned her family in Czechoslovakia. Otherwise they wouldn't have known the outcome because her name was never mentioned in Czech newspapers. Then one night Martina told her excited family she'd be meeting Chris Evert in the finals. Chris was #1. She'd already won the Wimbledon title twice, and she'd beaten Martina in twenty-three of their twenty-nine matches over the years.

They played their usual games in the finals: Chris at the base line, Martina volleying from the net. They played without the temper tantrums that crowds expected at this high level of tennis. With Evert–Navratilova, crowds witnessed sweet moments, including this one in the second set: Chris hit a ball that struck Martina in the head. Martina fell down, but got right back up, smiling. Chris met her at the net and gave Martina's head a gentle rubbing. Martina went on to win that set.

After Martina won their match, they stood together beside the umpire's chair. Martina was waiting to be presented with her trophy. "How come you're not crying?" Chris asked her.

"Not in front of all these people."

"I did, the first time I won here," said Chris. "I can't believe it. I hit you in the head and you started playing better."

They both laughed. Martina accepted her trophy with a curtsy to the Duchess of Kent and went off to phone her parents. Mirek's dream—her dream—had come true.

The rankings at last showed Martina to be #1. As a sports superstar she was chased by reporters, film-makers, and other wheeler-dealers, who wouldn't leave her alone until her private life became their public news. She was also hounded by agents wanting her to advertise their tennis shoes and socks and rackets and courts. Sports fans hunted her out for autographs. She suddenly had tons more fan mail to answer, and her phone rang day and night.

Fame cost Martina time she needed to practice. Still, she hung on to her #1 ranking by beating Chris in five of their seven finals in 1979, including the finals at Wimbledon again.

On that beautiful day Martina's mother sat in the players' box watching Martina for the first time in four years. She'd been allowed by the government to leave Czechoslovakia. She'd brought Martina a box of homemade cookies.

Later in the year Martina's father, mother, and sister emigrated to America. Generous Martina bought them a house down the street from hers in Dallas, Texas. She gave them two cars, a bank account, and much of her time between tournaments. But only her sister, Jana, adjusted to life in America. Her parents were shy about their English and lonely when Martina left for the tour. Martina was sorry to leave, but she had a job to do: to win tennis games. The tour was her profession, not a childish hobby.

Truth to tell, she didn't get along with her parents as well as they'd all expected. She didn't like to be reminded of her bedtime. She wasn't used to being told how to improve her strokes. After all, she'd won Wimbledon, hadn't she?

Her parents were proud people. They soon grew tired of depending on Martina's income. They went back to Czechoslovakia to their own jobs and took Jana with them.

What a blow! Martina had gained and lost her family in a few short months. But generous to the end, she sent them $50,000 to buy a house with enough land around it for forty apple trees: an estate like her mother's original home.

"I wish I could drop in for a visit," Martina has told the world in interviews.

Her parents' coming and going, her fame and fortune—these left Martina little time to concentrate on tennis. And in 1980 her ranking slipped to #3.

5

Tennis at the Top

Life in the fast lane! Jet-set days and nights. At age twenty-four, Martina had it all.

She could quit tennis forever and retire to an estate of her own. Or she could continue to tour, bouncing around in the top rankings for years to come. Either way, she'd eventually be cast in bronze for the Tennis Hall of Fame.

Ho-hum. It all seemed so easy. What more could Martina want?

Not surprising to those who knew Martina best—her opponents—Martina wanted to play *even better tennis*. She wanted to discover her physical and mental limits. What sort of tennis could she play if she dedicated her life to being the greatest winner in the history of the game?

Martina had the talent.

She had most of the shots.

But in the past Martina rarely had had the willpower for long, hard, daily training without a coach's encouragement. Alone, she'd hit practice balls—and that would be that. Martina hated "boring" exercise that didn't take place in actual competition. She also hated diets.

If Martina hadn't made several new friends—athletes who promised to help her by putting her through their own tough discipline—she might never have gone beyond her inconsistent tennis of 1980.

One new friend was a professional basketball player.

"Martina? What is this? Aren't you supposed to be real good?" asked Nancy Lieberman when she got to know Martina and watched her blow a match because she was tired and made mistakes.

Nancy had been an all-American basketball player in college. She had been running three or four miles per game for years and thus had learned the importance of endurance in competition: when *her* legs wore out, she missed her foul shots.

Endurance, no matter what the sport, depends on muscle strength and on heart/lung fitness.

Driven by the fiery Nancy Lieberman, Martina began a program of weight lifting on the Nautilus, Cybex, Hydrogym, Total Gym, and on free weights. When Martina tried to slack off her lifting, Nancy egged her on with insults.

"Come on, Tini, that really stinks. Your attention span's like a baby's." Nancy wasn't afraid to be sarcastic. She was a superstar athlete herself.

They jogged together, two miles or more, three days a week. They jumped rope three days a week for about ten minutes each day. Martina did sprints: 110 yards, 220's, 440's, then warm-downs of 880 jogs—

every day. She did sit-ups, a hundred daily. She ran on a treadmill and rode a stationary bike.

"Boring, boring," she'd moan and complain.

Nancy would turn on the TV sports station for Martina to watch while she kept up her pace on the treadmill. Then Martina sprinted up fifteen stairs, down, up—fifteen times every day. She stood and pumped her arms as if she were sprinting as fast as she could.

"That drill is a killer," Martina claimed about the stationary arm-pumping. It had looked so easy on Nancy's training sheet for the day.

These off-court exercises were followed by on-court drills of running, back-pedaling, pivoting, and swinging the racket. Then hitting serves at targets on court. Then returning serves of varying speeds and spins. (Spin is the rotation of the ball as it travels forward.)

When Martina was ready to learn new tennis strokes and to polish her game tactics, she invited Dr. Renee Richards to coach her. She'd been friendly with Renee, a brainy player, on the Slims tour. Martina remembered how Renee had beaten younger, better players by taking advantage of their weaknesses. Renee found out these weaknesses by studying players for hours from a seat in the crowd. Over the years Renee had studied Martina's weakensses. Renee now took on the job of strengthening Martina's game.

She helped Martina develop a topspin backhand.

This spin, given to the ball by hitting it on its top surface, made the ball trickier to hit back. Renee also taught Martina a way to serve more powerfully. By jumping into her serve, Martina could blast the ball for a lot of aces. (An ace is a serve that the opponent cannot touch.) Renee also improved Martina's forehand volley.

After practice they sat down and made Martina's game plan together.

"Renee would tell me about my opponent's personality, her tendencies on court, so I could be ready for her when we played," Martina has said. She's quick to give her coach credit for her wins.

Sometimes during matches Martina would gaze up toward Renee and Nancy in the bleachers, as if to confirm the game plan. Then her opponents would gripe that Martina was getting illegal hand signals from her coaches. Martina denied it, and she was never officially warned by an umpire about these signals. Martina claimed her friends were merely waving to her to encourage her because the crowds now broke into frequent "boos" during Martina's victories.

Martina was expected to win every match, so she heard her share of rude remarks from the grandstands. The underdog heard the cheers. At tennis matches in America, the underdog is really the crowd's favorite.

Martina won fifteen of the eighteen tournaments she played in 1982. Sure, she missed hearing cheers for her booming serves and forcing volleys. But she was determined to be the greatest winner ever, and she had to pay the price.

Another price she paid was the loss of friendship with her opponents on tour. Nancy had convinced Martina that all her opponents were enemies. She told Martina to avoid them off court. Martina must stop all her playful chatter on the sidelines and her gossip in the locker room. If she stayed friendly with other players, she might give away points to them in games.

Martina no longer played doubles with Chris Evert; their serious rivalry in singles was the reason. Martina had also given up her doubles partnership with Billie Jean King. They'd won at Wimbledon in 1979, but B.J. was getting older, slower, and had permanent injuries. Martina decided to take on a stronger player for an unbeatable partnership.

"Martina decided to junk me," said Billie Jean. "She never said a word to me. . . . Months went by and never an explanation."

Explanation? Martina's victories were her answers to questions.

Touring the world without the friendship of other players would have been lonely for Martina if she'd not formed a new Family Navratilova. Nancy. Renee.

And later Martina's nutritionist, Robert Haas. He taught her to stop depending on diets to control her weight and instead to eat balanced meals. Dr. Haas stressed food that gave Martina energy and stamina. She ate more pasta, potatoes, vegetables, fruit, grains; she ate less meat, less butter, less whole milk and other fats. Her weight dropped and held at a slim size 8. (Dress size. Martina is five feet seven inches tall.)

"Nutrition will become important in athletic training," Martina tells kids who ask her about their tennis game.

Family Navratilova gave Martina the assurance that someone cared about her on tour. She welcomed other experts into her family, for the quickest way to Martina's heart was to help her improve her game. Rich Elstein, a reflex trainer, put Martina through drills for better balance and reaction time. Mike Estep, a player on the men's tour, took over as her practice partner and coach. Returning hits from a man gave Martina experience against an opponent many times stronger than the women she faced in tournaments.

Her power game became awesome. In 1983 she won sixteen of seventeen tournaments—eighty-six of eighty-seven matches. After she beat Andrea Jaeger to win her fourth Wimbledon (in 1983), Martina was asked, "Do you think you're just too good for the women?"

"I hope so. I want to try to make it as boring as I can," Martina answered.

In other interviews Martina has told the press she hasn't done anything that every woman player can't do. She means that if women players build up their muscles by lifting weights, they can hit tennis balls harder. And if they build their stamina by daily running, they'll be able to stay fresh through three grueling sets per match. Martina has claimed that women players have been unwilling to pay the price to win at sports in America, where having power and big muscles is considered unfeminine.

"Martina's overall fitness program will change the way women play tennis forever," Pam Shriver has predicted. She has been Martina's doubles partner and knows Martina's power game better than most. They won four Wimbledon doubles titles together, 1981–84.

Their matches as a team were pure fun for Martina, who had never forgotten the team spirit of her youthful ice-hockey games. Martina and Pam Shriver not only won tournaments together; they also earned a reputation as entertainers. They kept up a stream of nutty talk on court. They made witty comments after they'd flubbed shots. Their friendly partnership took some of the pressure off Martina to be always at her unbeatable best. In doubles, if Martina let up a little

on her shots, Pam bore down harder. Winning *and* losing became "memorable and touching" (Martina's words) when shared with teammate Pam.

In singles, Martina's drive to be the greatest remained constant. She played only to win. Her fans and the media expected it of her, adding more and more pressure as she won twenty-five matches in a row. She won thirty-five, forty-five, fifty. She won fifty-four without a loss.

Then, in January 1984, Martina lost to Hana Mandlikova ("Mond-lik-kova"), a young Czech who used to be Martina's ball girl back in Prague. (A ball girl picks up balls for players.) The amazing winning streak had been broken by a player from the very tennis program that Martina's prize money had once helped support!

Martina didn't explain the loss by claiming burnout from too many tournaments. She didn't give in to the frustration of losing by taking a long vacation. Not Martina. Nothing could distract her from her goal. She began a new streak in the next tournament she

played, and over the months of 1984 she built her streak to fifty matches won, then to fifty-five without a loss.

On the practice court she worked with Mike Estep for four hours daily. He hit to her as hard as he could and forced her to keep the rally going.

Martina's streak went to sixty-five, seventy.

At practice she returned Mike's drop shots, his chips, his lobs (balls hit high in the air), and his slices

(balls hit with sidespin). This variety of shots called on Martina to be creative in the way she sent the ball back to Mike.

Her reputation changed. She was more than a powerhouse. She was the most versatile shot maker in tennis. Her streak reached seventy-four matches—the longest streak in tennis history. The tennis world believed she was unbeatable when she flew to Australia for the Australian Open in 1984. She, too, expected to win her fourth Grand Slam event of the year. (Winning the Grand Slam of tennis means winning the French Open, Wimbledon, the U.S. Open, *and* the Australian Open.)

In Australia, wherever Martina appeared, crowds followed. They caused traffic jams around her sports car. They haunted her practice court. Martina signed more autographs than she hit tennis balls, according to Mike Estep. Fans begged Pam Shriver to get them Martina's autograph. Martina's press conferences drew more reporters than the prime minister drew for his speeches. Reporters shouted, "Can you be beaten?" to Martina, and "Who can beat you?" and "When will somebody beat you?"

They paid little attention to a young Czech player, Helena Sukova, daughter of Vera Sukova. As a little girl, Helena had watched her mother hit balls to Martina in Czechoslovakia.

Helena Sukova quietly moved into the Australian Open semifinals, where she met Martina on December 6, 1984. They battled each other with nearly identical weapons. Each had a rocketlike serve, a fine net game, and the courage to buckle down harder after losing a point. They differed in their abilities to concentrate. At times in their match Martina's mind was on the swirling wind. She'd always hated to play on windy days.

Helena beat Martina 1–6, 6–3, 7–5.

Australians expected Martina to be too stunned to talk about herself in defeat, but right away she let them know what would happen next in her career.

"I'll start from scratch," she said about her ended streak. "I still have a whole body, two arms and two legs." She went back into training in order to win hundreds more tournaments in future years. She remained determined to prove she was the #1 tennis player of all time.

Off court, Martina donated her time to organizing the Martina Youth Foundation. Her hard-won money paid for rackets, balls, court time, and tennis lessons for children who would not otherwise have been able to afford tennis as a sport. Martina herself gave lessons on inner-city courts around America, saying she hoped some of these very kids might play against her in future years on tour.

Martina's new families would stand by her on tour. Her first family would cheer her with their visits to America from time to time. But Martina—alone on her side of the tennis court—has made her dream come true:

"Once I knew there was a world out there that played tennis, I wanted to be the best."

And so she is!

ABOUT THIS BOOK

Wherever you are, you're close to Martina.

Let her coach you. In your library or bookstore there's her book, *Tennis My Way*. It teaches her strokes, tactics, skill drills, weight workouts, psych-ups, and her nutritional program. Try some of Martina's ways to improve your own game.

Rarely a month passes without a Martina match on TV. Watch it with *Tennis My Way* on your lap. Compare Martina's words to her actual moves on court. In this way you'll witness her next book developing before your very eyes.

Then, when the tour brings Martina near enough, go see her play. She's a living legend that you might want to write about yourself.

1. Notice what she does between games. That's the part you miss on TV because of commercials.

2. Tape-record her words to herself on court. She's often funny. Record the sounds of her hits. Compare this sound to yours.

3. After the match, snap a close-up photo.

During the past ten years I've seen Martina play many matches. I've listened to her in press conferences, noting that her mind and life are open and changeable. Because of this freshness, Martina continues to interest me.

R. R. K.